THE HALL OF

FAITH

A devotional based on Hebrews 11

Victoria Fletcher

Now faith is the substance of things hoped for, the evidence of things not seen. For by it the elders obtained that the worlds were formed by the word of God, so that things which are seen were not made of things which do appear.

Hebrews 11:1-3

Hoot Books Publishing
851 French Moore Blvd.
Suite 136 Box 14
Abingdon, VA 24210

THE HALL OF ==FAITH==

Wow! Wouldn't it be an honor to have your name in the hall of ==faith==?

For this devotional, I will be listing the names in the hall of ==faith== given in Hebrews 11. I will also be telling you a little about how they were able to have their name mentioned in the hall of ==faith==.

I hope you will enjoy reading this devotional. This is one of my favorite chapters to read in the Bible. I use the King James Version of the Bible for my studies and devotionals, but I will list the reference so if you prefer another version to study or read, you can read it in the one you prefer.

Thank you for choosing this devotional. Okay, off we go with all the names mentioned in the hall of ==faith== and how they got to be there.

Victoria Fletcher

1. Abel was the first person listed in the hall of faith because his sacrifice was better than his brother Cain's. For this reason, he was found righteous by God.

A brief summary of Abel's life is found in Genesis 4:1-16.

Cain and Abel were born to Adam and Eve in the Garden of Eden. Cain was a farmer and Abel was a shepherd (the first shepherd ever mentioned in the Bible- just a bit of Bible trivia for you.) When it was time for sacrifice, Cain brought some of the food he raised but Abel brought his very best of the flock. God considered Abel's offering worthy of sacrifice. This made Cain so jealous and angry that he killed his own brother. But God knew and he told Cain that his crops would no longer grow and he would just wander the earth. Cain ended up living in the land of Nod separated from his family and from God.

2. Enoch walked with God and pleased Him so Enoch made the list next.

A brief summary of Enoch's life is found in Genesis 5:21-24.

Enoch was the great-grandfather of Noah. He is of the lineage of Seth, Adam and Eve's son. Because Enoch walked with God and was faithful, God took him directly to heaven instead of Enoch having to die. This is incredible to me that Enoch was so faithful that God chose to take him to heaven and he didn't have to die an earthly death. It happened again but I won't spoil it by telling you who it was. I want you to find it on your own and see why God took him without an earthly death as well.

It is believed that 1st, 2nd, and 3rd Enoch were books of the Apocrypha that were not included in the Bible but talked more about his life.

3. Noah believed God's warning and followed His orders. Noah was righteous by faith.

A brief summary of Noah's life is found in Genesis 6-9.

God was sorry about His creation because they had become so wicked and evil. But he found one righteous man—Noah. God gave Noah orders to build an ark to house Noah, Noah's wife, Noah's sons and their wives, and animals of every kind to replenish the earth after the flood that God was going to send. People laughed at Noah because there had never been a flood before. They tried to get on the ark when the rains came, but God has closed the door to the ark. It rained for 40 days and nights, so everything was destroyed except the ark and all on board. After the flood, God told Noah that he would not destroy the whole world by water anymore. God put a rainbow in the sky as a sign of His promise.

4. Abraham was given the land of promise because he had remained faithful to God in all things.

A brief summary of Abraham's life is found in Genesis 12.

Because of Abraham's faith, God was going to make a covenant with him. God told Abraham to take Sarah, his wife, and Lot, his nephew, and all he owned and leave Haran. He was to travel to the promised land of Canaan that God would give His people. Abraham obeyed.

Don't you think it would have been hard to leave the only place you had known and go to another place with everyone and everything you owned and start again.

Abraham didn't hesitate. He gathered up his servants, animals, his wife Sarah, and his nephew Lot and headed out to Canaan, the land promised by God to be his and his families forever.

5. Sarah, Abraham's wife, trusted in the promise of a son in her old age and was found faithful.

A brief summary of Sarah's life is found in Genesis 21.

When Sarah was visited by angels and told she would have a son, she laughed because she was 90 years old. That definitely had to be God's blessing on her, don't you think?

With God, nothing is impossible. Sarah had her son and named him Isaac, which means laughter. I wonder if she named him that so she would always be reminded of her laughing when the angels told her she would have a son that would be heir to the promise God was giving Abraham.

6. Abraham is mentioned again because he was even willing to sacrifice his son, Isaac, when God tested him. His ==faith== was rewarded.

A brief summary of Abraham and Isaac is found is Genesis 22.

Abraham was given Isaac in his old age (he was 100 years old). He loved Isaac because he was Sarah's son and destined to be the fulfillment of God's promise to Abraham. But even Abraham's great love for Isaac did not keep him from obeying God when God called for Isaac to be sacrificed. Abraham was ready to obey God. When God saw Abraham's obedience, God kept Abraham from harming Isaac and provided a ram instead.

I think that had to be an awfully hard decision for Abraham to obey but his obedience and ==faith== in God ended up giving him a blessing beyond words.

7. Isaac had twin sons, Jacob and Esau.
    He was considered faithful just like his
    father Abraham.

A brief summary of Isaac is found in Genesis
27:30-40.

Isaac was blessed with two sons—twins.
They were named Esau (the oldest) and
Jacob.

Isaac gave them their blessing according to
what God told him.

Esau was Isaac's favorite but Jacob was his
mother, Rebekah's, favorite.

There is so much more to the story of these
two brothers. You need to read all of their
story in Genesis 24-27.

Esau gave up his birthright for a bowl of soup
when he was hungry and then gave up his
blessing when Rebekah overheard the plan
that Isaac had and rushed to get Jacob the
blessing instead. As you can imagine, Esau
was not happy about being deceived and
even threatened to kill his brother.

8. Jacob was Isaac and Rebekah's son. He had a son named Joseph that he blessed before Jacob died.

A brief summary of Jacob's life is found in Genesis 49:22-26.

Jacob believed his son Joseph had been killed when his brothers brought a bloodied coat to show Jacob. He knew it was the one he had made for Joseph.

Imagine his surprise when he finds out Joseph is alive and in Egypt overseeing things for Pharaoh. Jacob was able to give his sons their blessings before he died.

You've got to read all of this story. From the brothers plotting to kill Joseph because they were jealous to finally selling him to a caravan travelling to Egypt where Joseph was bought by Potiphar, the Pharaoh's assistant.

Joseph became second in command under Pharaoh and took care of the grain during the years of plenty so all the surrounding lands had enough during the years of famine. Boy, his brothers must have been surprised!

9. Joseph, Jacob's son, asked his family to take his bones with them when he died. The family had all moved to Egypt when they found Joseph alive.

A brief summary of Joseph's life is found in Genesis 37.

After Joseph's father, Jacob, died, Joseph asked his brothers to leave Egypt and take his bones with them. Joseph wanted to be buried in the promised land of Canaan that God had promised for the Israelites. Joseph was 110 when he died.

There is so much more to the story of Joseph and his brothers. I hope you will read all of the account. It is so hard to imagine the envy and jealousy they had toward their brother, even to the point of wanting him dead. But they changed after that and proved themselves worthy to Joseph when he saw them in Egypt. See how Joseph tricked them into finding out about his father and younger brother, Benjamin.

10. Moses has several entries in the hall of faith. He was a humble man and God used him in mighty ways (even when Moses said he could not do what God was asking.)

a. Hid in basket in Nile to escape being put to death by Pharaoh (Exodus 2:1-8)

b. Left Pharaoh's daughter who found him on the Nile (Exodus 2:11)

c. Left Egypt to be with the Israelites (Exodus 2:11-23)

d. Kept the Passover (Exodus 12)

e. Crossed the Red Sea to flee Pharaoh and his armies (Exodus 14-15)

f. Walls of Jericho came down (Joshua 6)

A brief summary of Moses' life is found in Exodus and Joshua. Joshua was the one that took the place of Moses after Moses died.

Moses believed in God and obeyed His commands. Many of the Old Testament stories are about Moses.

11. Rahab had started her life as a prostitute. But she had heard about the God of the Israelites and wanted to learn more. She hid the spies when they came to Jericho. She wanted her family and her to be spared when the city was destroyed.

A brief summary of Rahab's life is found in Joshua 1-2.

It's so nice to know that God can save a person and let wonderful things come out of their life. Rahab left with the Israelites and married one. She is actually in the lineage of Jesus Christ. Her husband was Salmon who was the father of Boaz who was the father of Obed who was the father of Jesse who was the father of David who was of the direct lineage of Jesus Christ.

It's amazing how God worked in Rahab's life to let her come to know God and be saved by the Israelites when her city was destroyed.

Here are some other names listed but not actually put into the hall of ==faith== because of the length it would have been to include all that these people of ==faith== did:

    a. Gideon- Judges 6-8: Judge and military leader that won a battle with only 300 men chosen by God to defeat the Midianites. He was ==faith==ful and obedient to God's will.

    b. Barak- Judges 4-5: Military leader that won a victory along with Deborah against Sisera, the Canaanite general. He was ==faith==ful, obedient, and a strong leader.

    c. Samson- Judges 13-16: Judge and warrior with superhuman strength that fought the Philistines. Even through his human weakness, God renewed his strength to kill thousands of Philistines, but he also lost his own life in doing so.

    d. Jephtha- Judges 11: He made a vow to God to sacrifice the first thing he saw if given the victory over the Ammonites. Unfortunately, that turned out to be his only child, his daughter. God realized his faith when he kept his word.

e. David- Samuel: David became king after Saul. He fought a giant named Goliath and won. His human nature caused him to sin, but he repented to God. God called David "a man after my own heart."

f. Samuel- 1 and 2 Samuel: Samuel was Israel's last judge, prophet, and priest. His mother, Hannah, had prayed for a son and God heard her prayer. Hannah agreed to dedicate Samuel to serve at the tabernacle with Eli. Samuel became God's messenger and obeyed God's command to anoint a king, even when he didn't want to. That shows true faith.

g. Major and Minor Prophets- last 17 books of the Old Testament. Just to mention a few: Isaiah and Jeremiah prophesied about the birth of Jesus Christ. Jonah found out you can't run from God's calling. He changed his mind about preaching to a sinful city after spending three days in the belly of a big fish.

One that wasn't mentioned that I had studied and found that I think he should have been included was Daniel. Read his book too and you'll see how his faith and prayers let him do amazing things even when he was captured as a young boy and taken to Babylon. A few of my favorites are the lion's den, the handwriting on the wall, and interpreting the king's dreams and becoming third in authority in the kingdom of Babylon.

Other Verses About Faith

1. Deuteronomy 7:9- Know therefore that the LORD thy God, the faithful God, which keepeth covenant and mercy with them that love Him and keep His commandments to a thousand generations.

2. Psalm 31:23- O love the LORD, all ye his saints: for the LORD preserved the faithful and plentifully rewardeth the proud doer.

3. Habakkuk 2:4b [also Galatians 3:11b]- The just shall live by faith.

4. Matthew 17:20b- If ye have faith as a grain of mustard seed, ye shall say unto this mountain, Remove hence to yonder place; and it shall remove and nothing shall be impossible unto you.

5. Mark 4:40- Why are ye so fearful? How is it that ye have no faith?

6. Mark 11:22- Have faith in God.

7. Luke 7:50- Thy faith hath saved thee; go in peace.

8. Luke 16:10a- He that is <mark>faith</mark>ful in that which is least is <mark>faith</mark>ful also in much.

9. Luke 17:5- The apostles said unto the Lord, "Increase our <mark>faith</mark>."

10. Luke 18:8b- When the Son of man cometh, will he find <mark>faith</mark> on the earth?

11. Acts 11:24- For he was a good man and full of the Holy Ghost and of <mark>faith</mark>: and much people was added unto the Lord.

12. Romans 3:22- Even the righteousness of God which is by <mark>faith</mark> of Jesus Christ unto all and upon all them that believe: for there is no difference.

13. Romans 3:28- Therefore we conclude that a man is justified by <mark>faith</mark> without the deeds of the law.

14. Romans 4:5- But to him that worketh not, but believeth on him that justifieth the ungodly, his <mark>faith</mark> is counted for righteousness.

15. Romans 4:13- For the promise, that he should be the heir of the world, was not to

Abraham or to his see through the law, but through the righteousness of faith.

16. Romans 4:20- He staggered not at the promise of God through unbelief; but was strong in faith, giving glory to God.

17. Romans 5:1- Therefore being justified by faith, we have peace with God through our Lord Jesus Christ.

18. Romans 5:2- By whom also we have access by faith unto this grace wherever we stand and rejoice in hope of the glory of God.

19. Romans 10:17- So then faith cometh by hearing and hearing by the word of God.

20. 1 Corinthians 2:5- That your faith should not stand in the wisdom of men, but in the power of God.

21. 1 Corinthians 13:13- And now abideth faith, hope, and charity, these three; but the greatest of these is charity.

22. 2 Corinthians 5:7- For we walk by faith, not by sight.

23. Galatians 3:24 For we are all the children of God by faith in Christ Jesus.

24. Galatians 5:5- For we through the Spirit wait for the hope of righteousness by <mark>faith</mark>.

25. Galatians 6:10- As we have therefore opportunity, let us do good unto all men, especially unto them who are of the household of <mark>faith</mark>.

26. Ephesians 2:8- For by grace are ye saved through <mark>faith</mark>: and that not of yourselves; it is the gift of God.

27. Ephesians 6:16- Above all, taking the shield of <mark>faith</mark>, wherewith ye shall be able to quench all the fiery darts of the wicked.

28. 2 Timothy 4:7- I have fought a good fight, I have finished my course, I have kept the <mark>faith</mark>.

29. Philemon 1:6- That the communication of thy <mark>faith</mark> my become effectual by the acknowledging of every good thing which is in you in Christ Jesus.

30. 1 John 5:4- For whatsoever is born of God overcometh the world; and this is the victory that overcometh the world, even our <mark>faith</mark>.

I especially love this last verse. In today's world, Satan is adding to his army daily. We as believers in the Lord Jesus Christ need to be telling others about Jesus and the way to eternal life. I am so glad that my faith will give me victory over the world.

I hope all of you have faith and remain faithful and obedient to God. We don't know when the time will be that Jesus will come back for His believers. We know it <u>will</u> happen and we should be obeying God's Word and letting our lives be a witness to others so that they may know Him before it is too late.

Forever obedient and believing

Always trusting in God's Word

Increasing our faith daily

Telling others about Jesus Christ

Heaven waits for those who believe

About the Author

Victoria Fletcher was a teacher in the Washington County Virginia School System. She taught Sunday School, VBS, and children's choir at First Baptist Church in Damascus, Virginia for 43 years. She retired from teaching and took the secretary job at First Baptist Church. She now owns her own publishing company, Hoot Books Publishing, where she helps other authors prepare their books for publishing (mainly self-publishing).

She loves reading her Bible daily and has been excited to learn inductive Bible study over the last few years. She is president of the Appalachian Authors Guild, member of the Lost State Writers Guild, member of the Virginia Writers Club, and a member of the Writers & Readers Day committee.

Other Devotionals by the Author

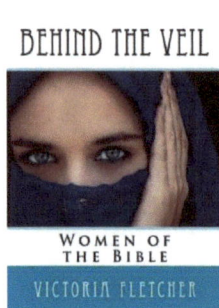

BEHIND THE VEIL

WOMEN OF THE BIBLE

VICTORIA FLETCHER

Getting Back on Track

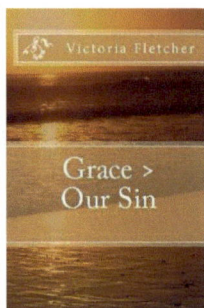

Victoria Fletcher

Grace > Our Sin

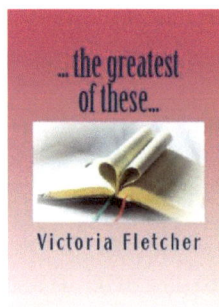

... the greatest of these...

Victoria Fletcher

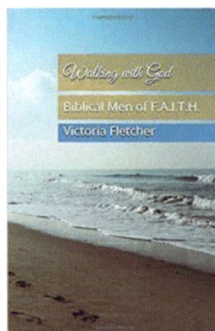

Walking with God

Biblical Men of F.A.I.T.H.

Victoria Fletcher

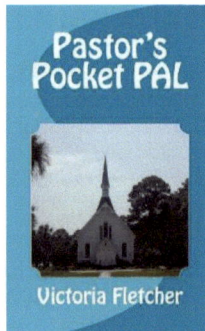

Pastor's Pocket PAL

Victoria Fletcher

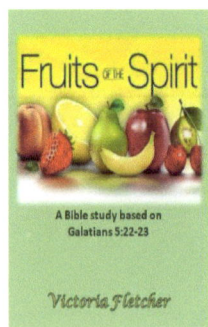

Fruits of the Spirit

A Bible study based on Galatians 5:22-23

Victoria Fletcher

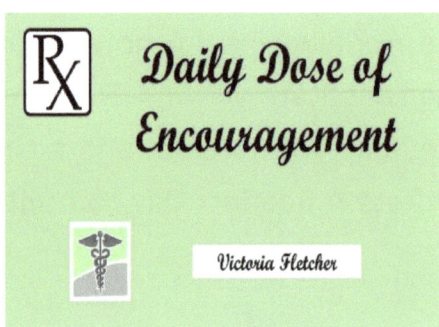

℞ Daily Dose of Encouragement

Victoria Fletcher

Other Books by the Author

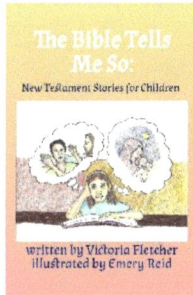

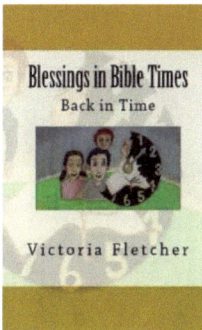

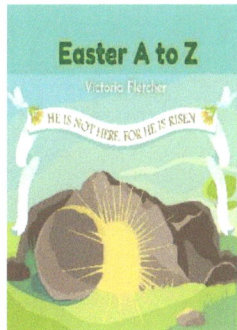

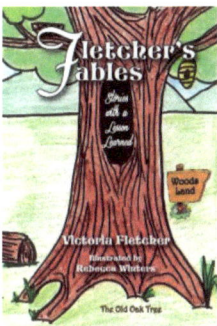

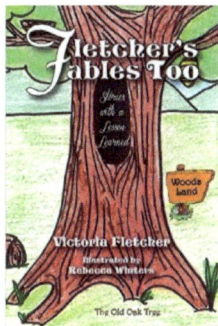

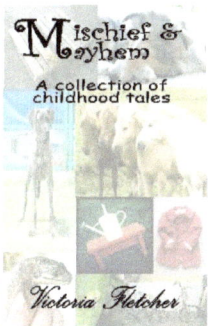

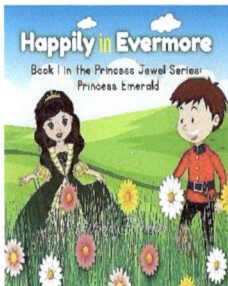
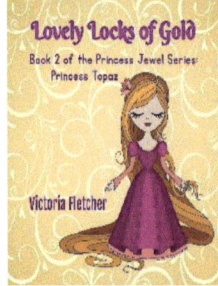

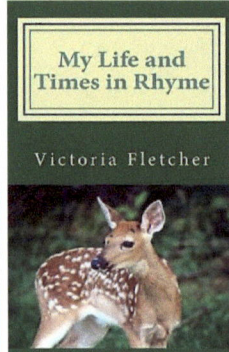
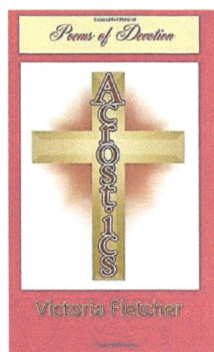

Coming Soon

Book 4 in the
Princess Jewel Series-
The Glass Slipper

If you are interested in getting any of my books, please check them out on my website: victoriafletcher.biz.

You can email me with an order at vfletcher56@gmail.com.

Once payment is received, I will ship your books or meet you if you are local to Abingdon, Virginia.

The books are available on Amazon except for the spiral bound perpetual calendar, "Daily Dose of Encouragement." It is only available through me personally.

Buying directly from me helps with the costs of printing the books since royalties are very small when purchased through Amazon. Thank you for considering my books.

Hope you've enjoyed this walk through the Hall of Faith. I'd love to hear from you. vfletcher56@gmail.com

www.ingramcontent.com/pod-product-compliance
Lightning Source LLC
Chambersburg PA
CBHW041810040426
42449CB00001B/44